Marston House

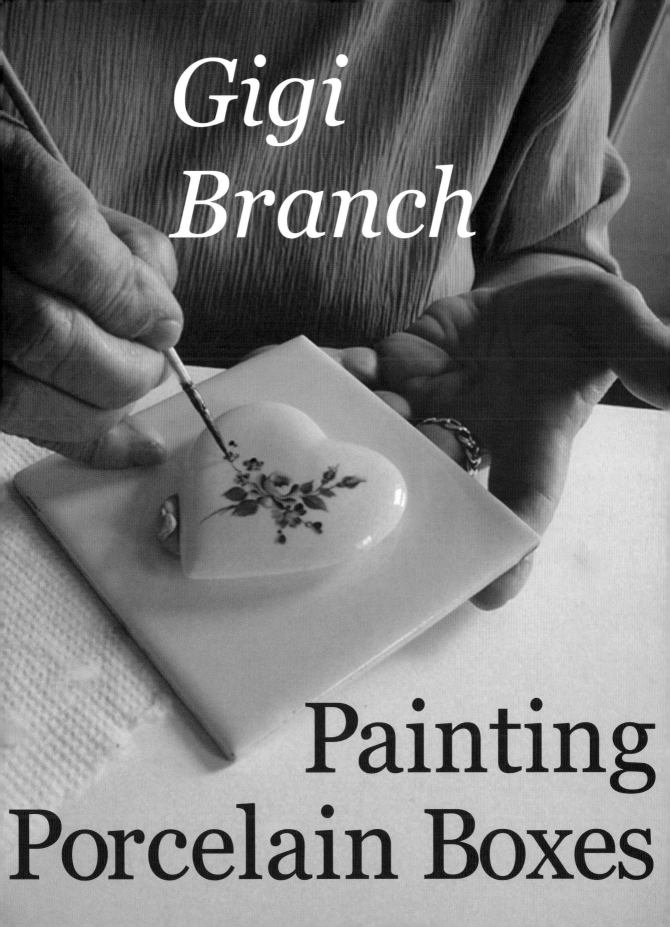

Gigi Branch

Painting Porcelain Boxes

Published in 2004 by Marston House
Marston Magna, Yeovil, BA22 8DH

ISBN 1 899296 23 9

**British Library
Cataloguing-in-Publication data**
A catalogue record for this book is available
from the British Library

*I dedicate this book to my
grandchildren Maisie and Sam*

Photography by Alphabet & Image Ltd

Printed in China by Regent Publishing Services

Contents

Introduction

I started china painting at the age of 15, going straight from school to the Paris atelier (studio) of Le Tallec, where I became part of a team of about twelve painters and including four apprentices. There I learned the traditional European style of decoration, using the quick drying medium of fat oil and turpentine. I was shown by my teacher, M Marchand, how to mix the colours, fill the brush, and to paint the different flowers in order to create a bouquet on the porcelain. I also learned various techniques such as laying a ground, raised work, gilding, etc, working on best quality Limoges porcelain.

I was delighted recently to find a photograph of one of my 'apprentice pieces', which I probably painted in the mid 1950s, illustrated in a big guide book for collectors of Limoges porcelain. It is apparently now in an American collection.

Largely because of my two books, *Painting on China in the French Style*, and *Painting Birds on China*, written since I came to work in England, I have been recognised as a specialist in the traditional European technique of china decoration, and this has resulted in invitations to seminars and demonstrations all over the world, which I much enjoy.

I have always preferred to decorate small pieces, and the small hinged Limoges boxes are amongst my favourites. I know many china painters share my passion, and this prompted me to produce this book of designs. I hope you enjoy it and find it useful.

Gigi

Tools and materials

Limoges boxes

A beautiful eighteenth century Meissen hinged box - an insipiration to all china painters!

Although many people think of Limoges boxes as porcelain boxes closed with a metal hinge, many other kinds of boxes are produced in Limoges, in south-central France, and indeed a wide range of porcelain has been manufactured there for over two centuries. Nearby sources of china clay and kaolin led to the opening of a hard-paste, or porcelain, factory in 1771, and in 1784 this factory was acquired to add to the production of the royal Sèvres works. The decoration of the two types of ware were similar, enormously popular and widely collected, reaching a peak in the period of Louis XVI. During this time the shapes and quality of the ware, and the beauty of the hand-painted decoration were breathtaking, as the many examples in the world's museums bear witness. By 1797 Limoges also became a mass exporter of porcelain, under the name of Haviland ware, to the United States.

Today only a few large factories remain, and the decoration is mainly done with transfers ('decal'). The lack of apprentices has led inevitably to the loss of qualified and experienced painters, and the few small factories, mainly family concerns, produce porcelain of very mixed quality. To bear the famous *Limoges France* mark beneath the clear glaze, porcelain must be produced within the small Haute Vienne region, of which Limoges is the capital. If they are painted by hand, there will be a mark - *peint main* - inside or on the base.

Above: blanks.   Below: the Limoges mark.

The time has passed when every piece was decorated at the place of production, and now plain
white porcelain can be purchased and decorated
elsewhere - to the advantage of porcelain
painters. The hinges and metal clasps are also
made at specialist centres. As the boxes vary
minutely in thickness, each metal frame is fitted
by hand and is unique to its box.

There are many 'Limoges style' boxes on the
market, but they can be easily recognised by the
lack of the Limoges stamp and by the width of
the metal covering the inside rim of the box -
mass produced to accommodate slight variations in thickness of the porcelain. These boxes
undoubtedly do lack the elegance and fineness
of the genuine article, but they are cheaper.

If you are trying to buy a decorated Limoges
box, beware of the words *rehaussé main* - this
means the the box is decorated with a transfer,
and a few strokes of enamel have been added,
but again, this method of production will be
reflected in a lower price.

Blanks and boxes

Shiny white glazed ware which has been fired in
a kiln to about 1300°C/2370°F is called a blank
in china-painting circles. It may be bone china
or porcelain, and slightly translucent, and is not
to be confused with earthenware, which is made
to a lower temperature, is completely opaque
and should not be used.

Porcelain has a hard glaze and if the colour we
paint on is applied too thickly it might chip off

after firing. Bone china has a softer glaze and will accept a thicker layer of paint. If you are not confident of your skill, start on a bone china box before trying porcelain. The designs we apply over the glaze are fired at a maximum of 850°C (1562°F) to allow the fusing of the enamel paint with the glaze and make the decoration permanent.

I have chosen in this book to decorate Limoges hinged boxes, but all the designs can be adapted to fit various blanks of the same shape, without hinges, made of bone china or porcelain. Blanks are now available in a very wide variety of shapes and sizes, and a list of major suppliers will be found at the end of this book.

When you purchase a Limoges box for decoration, it will come in three pieces - base, lid and metal fitting. Before taking off the metal frame it is important to mark with a dot of colour or pencil the position of the hinge or the front clasp on both the porcelain parts, so you are sure of getting your design facing the right way. Each hinge is specific to its box and it is important not to muddle up hinges and boxes, even if they are exactly the same shape. If you do, you may find that after all your hard work you have no hinge to fit the box. So, if you are working on several boxes of the same shape at one time, use a different colour reference mark on each box. It will save you a headache later on - believe me, I speak from experience!

Once you have glued on the metal frame it cannot go back into the kiln. So only when you are completely happy with your painting should you stick the metal frame to the box with epoxy glue, applied with a tooth pick or cocktail stick.

Equipment and workplace

Many of you will already have your workplace organised and be equipped with all you need, but for those who are not so experienced, here is the basic kit you need to paint in the techniques illustrated in this book. Again, major suppliers will be found at the end of the book:

genuine turpentine for grinding and for thinning the powder paints as well as for rinsing brushes.

fat oil of turpentine for mixing paints.

clove oil to slow down the drying time of the mixed paint.

alcohol or methylated spirits to clean the china before you start painting.

resist, also called *masking fluid* used to reserve an area for painting later, after a surrounding colour has been applied.

white ceramic tile or glass square to use as a palette for mixing colours, and to practise on - it is useful to have several.

palette knife with supple blade for grinding powder paint.

graphite pencil, such as Stabilo 8008, specially made to write on glass, ceramic and plastic.

fibre tip permanent marker pen to mark hinge position. Again, make sure it is one which will write on china or glass.

pen holder and mapping nibs to draw fine designs or outlines.

tracing paper and graphite paper for copying and transferring designs to china (carbon paper will not work).

stylus (blunt-ended tool) for transferring the tracing to the china.

Some of the basic tools, including pipette, marker pen, black and white stabilo pencils, palette knife, pen and stylus, small quantities

of powder paint (in stacking containers for travelling), methylated spirits, turpentine and fat oil and a ceramic tile.

pipette (dropper) for adding small quantities of turpentine to the paint.

icing (powder) sugar to mix with paint and water for quick-drying pen work.

cotton wool and silk to make pouncing pad for groundlay work.

synthetic cosmetic sponge, cotton buds and tooth picks (or cocktail sticks) for cleaning off paint.

banding wheel (not essential for most boxes)

re-usable adhesive putty (such as Blu-tack) for securing the box on a tile when it is too small or difficult to hold and paint.

burnishing sand, fibreglass burnisher or pad for polishing matt gold.

powder paints (technically known as on-glaze enamel) in various colours.

matt gold, and thinners to dilute it when it gets sticky. It becomes shiny when burnished.

kiln, or access to one shared with other painters.

11

brushes (most of these can only be obtained from specialist suppliers - don't try to buy them from the average art shop). I use French quill brushes (made of squirrel hair):

short pointer brush, also called a rose brush or grain of wheat, No. 4 (4 mm diameter, 8 mm long), or No. 3 (3 mm diameter, 6 mm long) for roses and other flowers with broad petals, and leaves.

long pointer No. 2 (2 mm diameter, 15 mm long) for most other flowers and for details.

two other brushes the same size, one used exclusively for gold the other exclusively for relief enamel.

pointer kept exclusively for applying resist.

flat synthetic brush for applying groundlay.

long square floppy brush for brushing off powder.

square shader No. 8 for feathering.

Make sure your workplace is well lit, preferably from the left if you are right-handed, and vice versa. An armrest is useful, and a large magnifying glass on a stand or magnifying spectacles if your sight is not that good - these boxes are very small, and the designs even smaller!

Above, from left to right: soft square shader, long floppy brush, synthetic flat brush, long thin pointer (for relief), short pointer (for resist), pointer (for gold), long thin pointer (for flowers), rose brush No. 4 and rose brush No. 3 (for roses and broad petals).

Support your painting arm on the table, and brace the hand or tile holding the porcelain under the table edge, for maximum steadiness. Make sure all the materials you need - mixed paint and turpentine for cleaning the brushes - are within easy reach.

Basic techniques

Mixing paint

Put the quantity of paint powder on a mixing tile and add a few drops of turpentine with the pipette. Crush the paint with a circular motion of the palette knife until it is smooth but damp.

Add a little fat oil on the end of your knife and mix well (as a guide, the amount of oil should not be more than half the amount of powder, but add a little at a time as it is easier to remedy too dry a mixture than too oily a one).

To test the consistency, stroke a pointer brush gently towards you, with the bristles opened flat, through the paint. Make parallel stokes in the same direction on a practise tile, and observe the shading created as the brush load is emptied.

Below: adding turpentine with a pipette to the paint powder. A small quantity of fat oil is also on the tile. Top: crushing the paint with the palette knife. Right: as the brush load empties a shading gradient is created.

The paint should dry quickly. If the colour spreads like watercolour, it is too wet and you can get rid of the excess moisture by breathing on it (a 'Ha' breath, without the sound). If the paint dries on the palette and reverts to powder, there is not enough oil to bind it together, so add a little fat oil.

13

If the strokes run together with no shading and are very shiny there is too much oil. Add more powder and loosen the paint with turpentine.

The mixture should be soft and creamy, and the brush should open when filling without any effort.

Addition of a little turpentine makes paint which has dried on the tile usable again. You can even start again the next day with paint that has been resurrected in this way, although I always prefer to mix it freshly each time.

You will come across the terms open and closed mediums in china painting instructions. Most of the designs in this book use a closed medium, which is quick drying and consists of turpentine and fat oil. You use this when you want the brush stroke to stay exactly as you have painted it, and of course this does not allow for changes. Most of the European style of flower painting uses this medium. An open medium consists only of oil, and it does not dry at all, going into the kiln wet. This is used to mix paint when you want a very thin coat which can then be smoothed over with feathery strokes of a soft quill brush, as in the malachite or wood-effect boxes (pages 46 and 82).

Brush strokes

In the traditional European style of painting the brush strokes are very important. As the medium is quick drying there is no possibility of moving the paint when it has been applied.

Always fill the brush when it is open, and bring it back to a point as you draw it towards you.

Hold the brush nearly vertical and press it down until it is squashed open before easing the pressure as you draw the brush down, finishing on the point of the brush, making a stroke like an exclamation mark.

Paint will quickly dry on the palette but a little turpentine will loosen it again. For the same reason, rinse your brush frequently in turpentine.

Right: practise strokes until you are confident.

Top two rows: using a pointer brush practise petal and daisy shapes, creating shading as you empty the brush load. Each petal is one brush load.

Third row: fill the rose brush by entering the paint on the tile from the right, in a curved 'C' motion. Make the same move as you empty it on to the porcelain, creating shading in the ball-like shape. Loading the brush the same way, add petals on the right, but load the brush from the left for the petals on the left hand side. To paint the heart, turn the rose upside down and, starting at the centre, pull increasing semi-circles from the same side.

Fourth row: use a pointer brush for tulips.

Fifth row: a variety of leaves painted with a pointer brush. The central rose leaves are made with a series of 'C' strokes of decreasing size.

Sixth row: rose buds, forget-me-nots and bells.

Below: the correct angle to hold the brush.

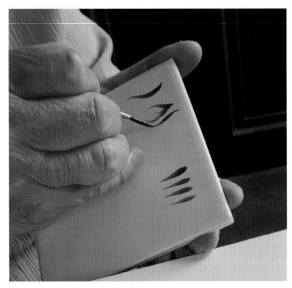

Transferring a design to the box

First place a piece of tracing paper over your pattern and copy with a dark felt tip or pen. Then position this tracing on the desired area of the box and secure at the top with a small piece of masking tape. Make sure you have placed the design in the right position in relation to the back of the box - where you have marked the hinge position. Slide the graphite paper, matt side down, beneath the tracing and secure with another tape at the bottom. Now follow the pattern with the stylus, conveying it on to the porcelain beneath. If you do not have graphite paper, you can make your own by scribbling on the reverse of the tracing with a graphite pencil.

Some people draw their designs and divisions with a marker pen and are not distracted by the strong outline. Others prefer the softer graphite line.

First copy your design onto tracing paper (below). Use graphite paper or cover the reverse of your tracing with graphite (top right). Use a stylus carefully to copy the design onto the porcelain (bottom right).

16

Paper dividers can be bought with circles divided into different numbers of equal segments. This one shows 4, 8 or 16 segments. They are helpful for marking equal divisions on any piece of porcelain, from a thimble to a plate.

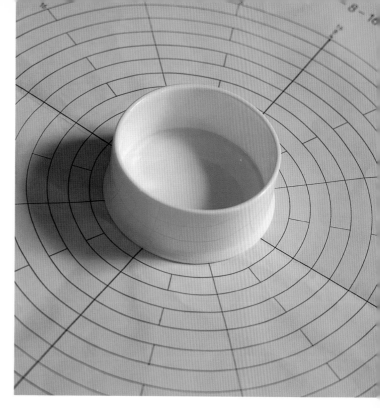

Below: drawing a simple border. Note the position of the pencil and the middle finger, braced against the edge of the box lid. Bottom: tracing around a simple shape to reserve a space for the design.

Groundlay

This is the term for the solid coloured area which usually frames your design, but it can also cover the whole piece.

Grounding must be completed and fired before you move on to the design, which will be fired at a lower temperature.

If the groundlay is to be a frame you have first to reserve a space for the design by drawing a border with a graphite pencil. If it is to follow the shape of the box, it can be done simply by holding your graphite pencil firmly in one hand, with its tip in contact with the surface and another finger braced against the edge, and rotating the piece steadily with your other hand.

If you want a fancy or undulating border you will need to trace its shape on tracing paper, make a stencil by cutting out the shape, stick it lightly on to your box and trace round the edge.

Next you must paint resist (masking fluid) around the inside of the border, on the area which will remain white and contain your design. This will protect it from the groundlay colour. Next apply the resist thickly around

17

the reserved area with a brush kept specially for the purpose. Rinse the brush straight away in water, as it is very hard to clean once it dries. When dry peel off the resist before firing.

Red resist is water-soluble, dries rapidly and is used with oil-mixed colour for wet or dry groundlay. Green resist is acetone based and is needed when the colours are mixed with water (or milk). If red resist were to be used here it would not form a barrier to the groundlay, which would penetrate into the reserved area.

Wet groundlay (painted or sponged on to the porcelain) is used for most of my designs, but sometimes it is more appropriate to dry ground-lay a piece. I did this for the matt colours used in the Vesta box (page 30) and the Pill box with scrolls (p. 33).

Wet groundlay: Mix your chosen dry colour with a few drops of turpentine and grind it thoroughly with a palette knife. When it looks like fine wet sand can you add the fat oil, in approximately the same quantity as the powder you started with. Mix well and loosen with 2 or 3 drops of clove oil to slow down the drying time, so you can complete the coat in one go.

I use a synthetic square shader brush to put the paint on, in rapid long strokes, then smooth the whole surface with the sponge in quick light pats, without stopping too long in one place, until it looks even.

Let it dry, and then pull off the resist by lifting one edge with a tooth pick. Clean off any smudges of colour with cotton wool and fire at 800°C/1470°F for bone china, 825°C/1515°F for porcelain. You might want to apply a second coat for a darker shade, and then fire again at the same temperature.

Dry groundlay Apply fat oil slightly diluted with turpentine with a flat brush to the area to be coloured. Straight away pounce the area (with a cotton wool ball wrapped in two layers of silk) until the surface is tacky, matt and even.

Sprinkle the powder colour evenly over the oil, pushing away the excess with cotton wool or a soft brush. It will stick only where the oil is, and

not where the box is to remain white.

Peel off the resist, clean and fire at 800°C/1470°F for bone china, 825°C/1515°F for porcelain.

Top: fat oil being brushed on the area to be painted with the groundlay colour. Below: a pouncing pad used to smooth the oil before the powder is applied.

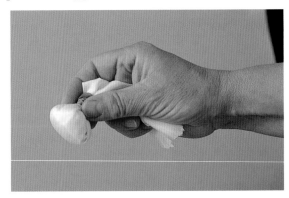

Malachite

Malachite is a naturally occurring bright green mineral rock, based on copper, with a characteristic rosette pattern. The box shown here is based on the natural colour and appearance of the stone, but there is nothing to prevent you using the same technique for a purely decorative pattern in any colours you choose and not as a copy of a real stone. Any kind of vibrant colour softly brushed on top of darker shades will give you the chance to create a totally unique design. The 'rosettes' could even be replaced with stripes, dots, etc. Using shades of brown you can create the effect of rings in cut wood. The possibilities are endless.

First draw the rosette patterns with a pen in at least two shades of your chosen colour. Then, using a thin pointer brush, apply shades of colour in a thin wash between the lines of the rosettes. These coats should be darker than the top coat, which is applied over the whole dried design in feathery strokes with a square shader brush. Fire at 800°C/1470°F.

A box painted in the malachite pattern and colours, complete with two perfume bottles.

Below: after the groundlay has been applied the resist is lifted off with a toothpick.

Firing

To fix the paint to the glaze permanently, you will need to fire the china in a kiln - an ordinary cooker oven will not do as it will not reach the required temperatures. Suppliers of kilns are shown on pages 85 and 86.

Firing temperatures vary for different techniques and stages - higher for groundlay (825°C/1515°F), lower for the painted designs and relief, and for gold which is painted on white (780°C/1435°F), but if gold is painted over colour it needs to be lower again at 700°C/1435°F, or it will sink into the colour and stay dull.

The individual design instructions give firing temperatures for each stage.

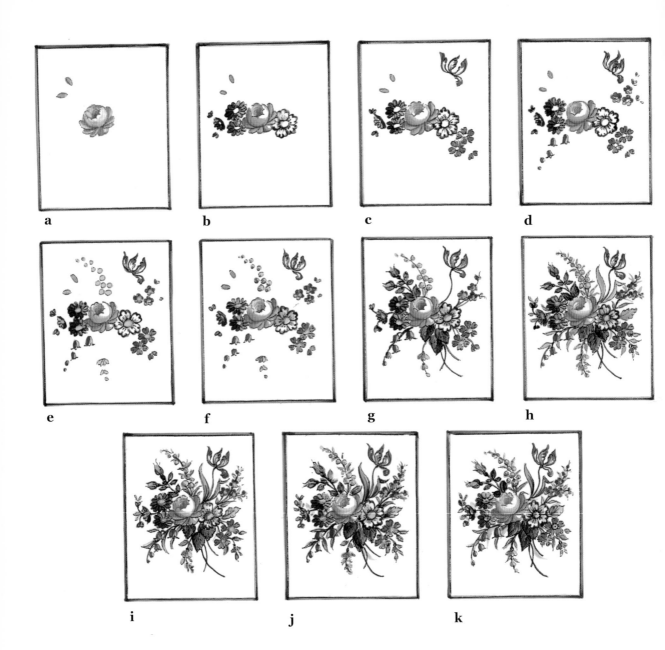

a   b   c   d

e   f   g   h

i   j   k

Painting a bouquet

This spray of flowers can be copied, or altered by the addition or deletion of various flowers, changes of colour, etc.

Because the turpentine and fat oil mixture dries fast, I mix and work one colour at a time, starting with the pink rose and its buds **(a)**, as it is almost always the most important flower in the arrangement. I use the rose brush for the rose and for any wide petal or leaf, and the long thin pointer for the rest.

Next comes violet for any important flower close to the rose, for tulips and daisies **(b)**; then red for other important flowers **(c)**. Blue is next, for forget-me-nots and bells **(d)**. Then yellow for any remaining flowers **(e)**, as well as the centre of others, except for yellow daisies which take a blue-green. Light brown **(f)** is used to shade the yellow flowers and the mixture needs to be a little more oily to work over the dry yellow paint. Dark green **(g)** is used to paint rose leaves with little 'C' strokes, and the rose buds, plus the stems of all the other flowers. Light green **(h)**, painted as a light wash, fills the bouquet with other leaves, and then dark green again to add veins to the light green leaves **(i)**. Blue green **(j)**, in a slightly more oily mixture, is applied as a very thin wash over the top half of the light green leaves, and to add some shadow leaves in the background if needed.

Finally, black is mixed with icing sugar and water (2 parts paint, 1 part sugar) to ink consistency, for penning tiny dots **(k)** around the yellow centres of flowers, and to sign work beneath the base.

Marble-effect background

This is a very easy and effective way to make a border, a background or to cover a less-than-perfect groundlay.

Still using the drying medium of turpentine and fat oil, I separately mix two tones of the same colour and first apply the lighter tone roughly, in patches, leaving some of the white porcelain showing through. I then do the same with the next colour, sponging it over quickly at random.

Straight away, before it dries, clean out some veins diagonally and unevenly across the colour with a thin liner or long pointer brush, just damp with turpentine, rolling it between your fingers as you work down.

Mix both colours on the tile and sponge on patches of the lighter tone (below). Then sponge on the darker tone (right). Veins are cleaned out through the paint with a thin liner brush (right, below).

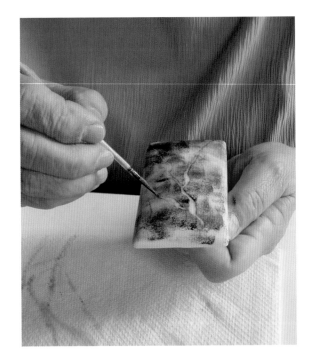

Relief enamel

Relief does add an extra dimension to your work, literally and in terms of impact, and is a very useful decorative tool. It can be left white, or painted over with gold, or it can be coloured at the mixing stage - only a minute amount of colour is needed as relief enamels tend to fire darker.

Relief enamel usually comes as a white powder, but can also be found ready mixed in water or oil-based medium, and applied with a tube and nozzle or a syringe.

If using the traditional method, mix the powder with a little fat oil and then thin out with turpentine until it 'strings' when you pull the brush through it. The mixture must stay in a pile on your palette and not spread out, or the same will happen to your stroke when you paint with it. If it is too runny, breathe on it (make a 'Ha' without the sound) until it tightens up.

Load a long pointer brush by pushing the brush away from you, lifting it at the same time, leaving it with a small tear drop of enamel at the end.

Practise by holding the brush vertically and depositing a blob of enamel on a tile: it should remain domed and not spread. If is is too spiky, it is too dry, so add a little oil. Repeat, making a succession of dots with one load, getting a gradual reduction in size. Try drawing the blob towards you to make petal shapes, and then leaf shapes and scrolls. Alphabet letters require practice - but some are easier than others, and come in hundreds of variations.

The enamel mix will dry naturally as you work so you may need to add a little turpentine to keep it manageable.

Fire relief enamels at 760°C/1400°F on a colour background, 780°C/1435°F on white.

Above: relief can be applied over groundlay colour as a decorative border and as leaves or buds, as here.

Do not forget :

Things that apply to all boxes illustrated

Before starting to paint a box, all blanks must be cleaned with alcohol or methylated spirits to remove all grease and finger marks. These could affect the end result, making it patchy when fired.

It is important to remember where the hinge fits at the back of the box, so you know where to place your design. The metal rim only fits one way, and you might find you have painted your design back to front when you come to glue the hinge and clasp on. Mark the position of the hinge on both parts of the box with a permanent marker pen. However, this will burn off in the first firing, so if you are doing groundlay before your design, put a spot of groundlay colour near the rim of the box (where it will be covered later by the metal) to again mark centre back.

Matt gold must be shaken vigorously before use to disperse the sediment of real gold through the liquid medium. Matt gold can be fired at 780°C/1435°F on white porcelain, but reduce temperature to 700°C/1290°F when it is painted over colour. After firing, matt gold should be polished with burnishing sand or a glassfibre tool.

After the last firing, the hinge must be glued to the base and lid with epoxy glue or 'super glue'. Keep the box open while drying, to avoid any risk of it sticking closed.

If the box is difficult to handle while painting, stick it with re-usable putty-type adhesive on a ceramic tile. This can even be placed in the kiln without harm to the box - the adhesive will turn to powder during firing.

Place a small amount of a re-usable putty adhesive such as Blu-Tack on two points of the rim and press down on a tile until it is firmly held. It is then easy to hold the tile while you paint the box.

One of the Fabergé eggs with gold filigree created for the Russian Romanov family.

Lattice ball

The shape of this piece inspired the decoration, based on a famous Fabergé egg.

Materials needed
turpentine, fat oil, icing sugar
relief enamel, matt gold, burnisher
rose brush No. 3, long thin pointer for leaves and details, long thin pointer for enamel, long thin pointer for gold
graphite pencil, pen, permanent marker pen
colours in order of use: light blue, yellow, light golden brown, light green, dark green, black

Using a paper divider, draw 16 equal divisions around top and base, starting at the hinge mark, and then extend these marks to the top and bottom, so the box is segmented, like an orange.

Draw a tiny circle about 1 cm across at the top, then draw another 4 lines horizontally around the lid and the base. This can be done freehand or by using a tape measure to mark dots about 0.5 cm apart on the vertical lines, and joining these around the box **(a)**. Accurate preparation is vital if you want to create a professional piece.

Using a turntable if needed, paint the first line of matt gold with the gold brush around the widest pencil ring on top and base, and the tiny top circle.

a

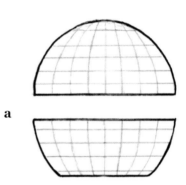

b

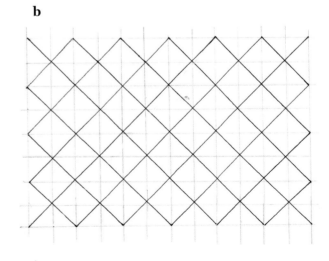

After the first firing

Now, freehand, paint diagonal gold lines by joining the corners of the pencil grid squares, from left to right and then right to left, to form the criss-cross pattern **(b and c)**.

When the gold is dry, mix the white relief enamel with turpentine and fat oil until it is stringy (see p. 23 for help), and apply dots at the intersections of the pattern **(c)**.

Fire at 780°C/1435°F.

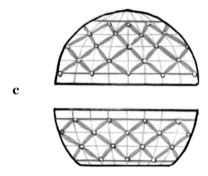

c

d

Mix light blue with turpentine and fat oil and paint a full forget-me-not flower (5 dots) with the rose brush in the upper part of the largest lozenges, followed by 3 dots and 1 dot buds in the smaller ones **(d)**. A few flowers can also be painted inside the base **(see opposite)**.

Mix yellow and fill the centre of each full flower. Underline the yellow with golden brown.

Mix light green and paint 2 long thin leaves under each flower. Then use dark green for stems and leaf veins.

Mix black with icing sugar and water and pen a tiny dot in each yellow centre. Sign your work under the base.

Using the gold brush filled with matt gold, cover the white relief dots and paint the scrolls and the line at the very base **(e)**. You can also add a small gold flower in the top circle and inside the lid. Fire at 780°C/1435°).

Polish the gold with sand or a fibreglass burnisher.

Left: after the second firing

e

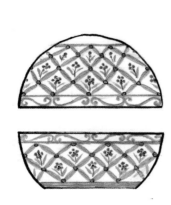

27

Square marbled box

Marbling is a very attractive technique, and works with a variety of colours. You must be careful to not overdo the veining - it takes a bit of practice to get it right. See page 22.

Materials needed
turpentine, fat oil, icing sugar, peelable resist
rose brush No. 3, long pointer No. 2, gold brush pen, cosmetic sponge, graphite pencil
gold, burnisher
colours in order of use: rose pink, ruby pink, violet, red, light blue, yellow, light golden brown, dark green, light green, blue green, black

Using the graphite pencil, draw the border on the lid and on the base where the marbling is to go. This is easiest if you first draw two squares within each other, and then draw the S-shaped curves between them.

Apply resist within the curved line on top and base, where it is to remain white **(a)**. For help with the groundlay technique see p. 17.

Mix the rose pink and ruby pink separately with turpentine and fat oil.

Dip the sponge into the rose pink and pad some uneven patches along the border of the lid and the reserved sides of the base. Repeat the process with the ruby pink.

Just damp the thin pointer brush with turpentine and, rolling it between your fingers as you draw it across the pink, clean some veins through the paint.

When dry, take off the resist, clean off any smudges and fire at 825°C/1515°F.

After the first firing

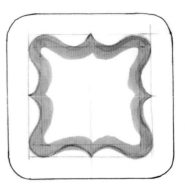

a

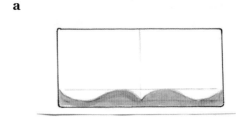

Paint the spray of flowers, one colour at a time **(b)**. For help with painting flowers, see page 21. You can add a rose inside the base, and a bud in the lid.

Mix black with icing sugar and water and pen dots in the centre of the flowers. Sign your work under the base and fire at 800°C/1470°F.

After the second firing

b

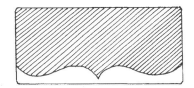

c

Paint the gold scroll inside the border on the lid and base **(c)** and the scrolls along the bottom of the base. Fire at 760°C/1400°F.

Burnish the gold with sand or a fibreglass burnisher.

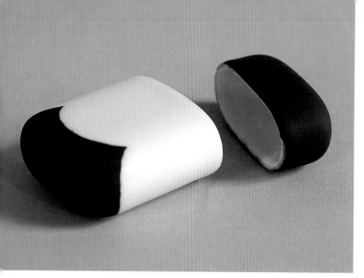

After the first firing

Vesta box

In Victorian times, Vesta matches were carried in flip-top silver or brass boxes, just like this one in shape - hence the name.

Materials needed
turpentine, fat oil, icing sugar, peelable resist (masking fluid)
relief enamel, matt black
graphite pencil, pen, permanent marker pen
rose brush No. 3, long pointer No. 2, resist brush, flat synthetic brush
pouncing pad (made with cotton wool covered in 2 layers of silk), cotton buds (Q tips)
colours in order of use: rose pink, violet, red, light blue, yellow, light golden brown, dark green, light green, blue green, black

With a graphite pencil divide the base into 4 vertical sections and then draw the curved line on front, sides and back **(a)**.

Apply masking fluid (resist) on the side of the line where it is to remain white **(b)**.

Apply fat oil, slightly diluted with turpentine, with the flat brush in long strokes on the reserved area. For help with the groundlay technique see p. 17.

Pounce (dab repeatedly) these areas with the silk pad until it is tacky, matt and even.

Sprinkle the matt black evenly over the oil, brushing away any excess with cotton wool or a soft brush.

Peel off the resist, clean any smudges on the white, and fire at 825°C/1515°F.

a

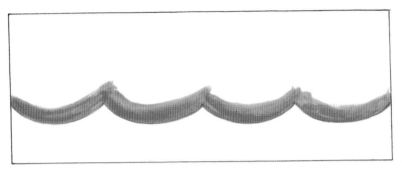

b

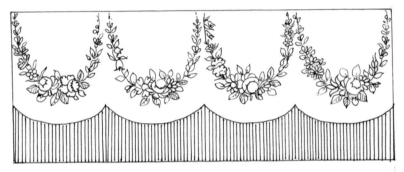

c

With the pencil draw the curve for the garland, about 1 cm from the black area at the base.

Mix the pink powder with turpentine and fat oil and paint a pink rose at the lowest point of each garland. Follow with the painting of the other flowers **(c)**, one colour at a time, in the usual order, ending with black, mixed with water and icing sugar, to pen tiny dots in the yellow centres of the flowers. Sign your work inside the box.

After the second firing

31

Mix the relief enamel with turpentine and fat oil until it 'strings' (see p. 23), and make dots on the black areas **(d)** with a long thin brush, loading anew for each dot. Fire at 780˚C/1435˚F.

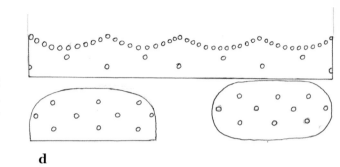

d

Pill box with scrolls

This elegant little box relies on its satin finish and relief pattern for impact. The platinum inside is a surprise!

Materials needed
turpentine, fat oil
relief enamel powder or ready-mixed enamel
pouncing pad made with cotton wool wrapped in 2 layers of silk, soft brush or cotton wool
long thin pointer brush for enamel, flat synthetic brush, pointer brush for platinum
white graphite paper or pencil, permanent marker
black metallic powder paint (also called satin)
bright platinum
small tile and re-usable putty adhesive

Because it is impossible to hold the box while completing painting I stick it on to a ceramic tile with adhesive putty at this stage (see page 24).

Put a small amount of fat oil on a tile with a minute amount of your powder black (to colour the oil so you can see where you are padding later) and check that you can work the flat brush through it. If it is too thick, add a little turpentine. For help with groundlay see p. 17.

Apply the oil with this brush all over both halves of the box, and then pad with small fast movements until it is matt and tacky.

Deposit a little pile of the metallic powder on the centre of each half of the box and then gently spread it over the whole surface with the soft brush until the oil cannot absorb any more. Brush off the excess with the soft brush or cotton wool. Clean off any stray colour inside and fire at 830°C/1526°F.

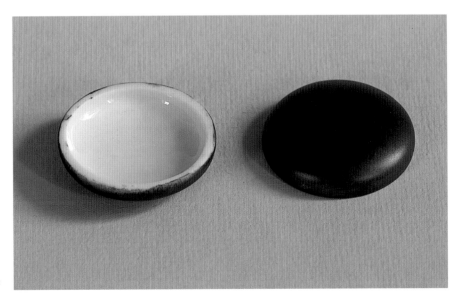

After the first firing

Trace the basic scroll pattern **(a)** on lid and base with the white graphite pencil or paper. A few alternative patterns are also shown here.

Mix the relief enamel with fat oil, adding a little at a time until a smooth, stiff mixture is

a

After the second firing

obtained, and then add a little turpentine until it just starts to 'string' (see p. 23). Mix it until you can pick up a small ball of the paste on the point of the thin brush without it leaving a peak in the mixture. Try to paint an exclamation mark on a tile as a test.

With the thin pointer brush follow the scroll pattern with the enamel, starting at the edges and working towards the centre. Fire at 780°C/1435°F.

Using a larger brush, kept for this paint, paint the insides of the box with platinum. Turn lid and base over and stick the rims on to the tile. (If at all worried about painting the inside and the outside at the same stage, fire at 740°C/1360°F before moving on to the next stage.)

Using a long thin pointer kept for this paint, cover all the scrolls with platinum.
Fire at 740°C/1360°F.

After the first firing

a

b

Oval box with rural scene

This was inspired by the scenes on eighteenth-century Meissen porcelain. Any country subject could look equally good, on this or boxes of other shapes.

Materials needed
turpentine, fat oil, icing sugar, alcohol or methylated spirits
short pointer brush (rose brush No. 4), long pointer brush No. 2
graphite pencil, pen and nib, marker pen
graphite paper and tracing paper (optional)
colours: light blue, pink, yellow, light golden brown, light green, blue green, dark brown, dark green, black

Trace the design with tracing paper and transfer to the box lid and base with graphite paper, or draw freehand with the pencil **(a and b)**.

Mix the colours separately with turpentine and fat oil, except for the last three, which will be used after the first firing.

Starting at the top of the scene, using the rose brush for the wide areas and the long thin pointer for the small details, paint a very light sky with blue.

Working your way down, now paint the rest of the scene very lightly with the correct colours, omitting dark brown and dark green.

Paint the flowers and insects on the base, but without the finer details.

Fire at 800°C/1470°F.

Strengthen the painting with the same colours as necessary.

Mix dark brown and dark green with turpentine and fat oil and add the details on the house, tree, stones, fence and grass.

With pink, add a few dots to suggest roses growing up the wall and around the front door.

On the base, add some shading to the pink flower and to the blue forget-me-nots if required.

With dark green, paint the stems and some veins on the leaves, with dark brown details on the insects.

Mix black with sugar and water and add a dot in the centre of the flowers, and sign your work under the base with the pen.

Fire at 780°C/1435°F.

Oblique design

Materials needed
turpentine, fat oil, clove oil
matt gold, icing sugar, peelable resist
rose brush No. 3, long pointer No. 2, resist
brush, flat synthetic brush, gold brush
graphite pencil, pen, permanent marker pen
cosmetic sponge, burnisher
colours in order of use: rose pink, violet, red,
light blue, yellow, light golden brown, dark
green, light green, blue green, black

With the pencil mark the diagonal lines separating the background colour from the white part containing the flowers.

Apply resist to the side of the line where it is to remain white **(a)**.

Mix your chosen colour for the groundlay with fat oil and turpentine, adding a few drops of clove oil to slow down the drying time. Apply rapidly in the reserved area with long strokes of the flat brush.

Smooth the colour all over with quickly with the sponge. For help with groundlay see p. 17.

Peel off the resist, clean up any smudges. Fire at 825°C/1515°F.

After the first firing

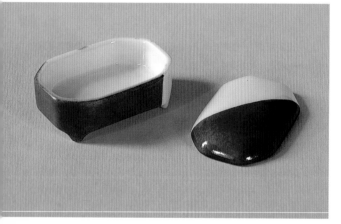

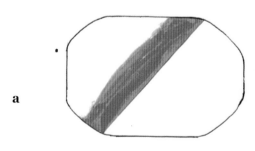

a

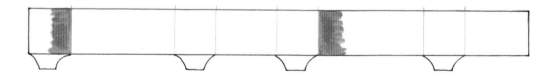

After the second firing

Paint the flowers in the spray and on the sides in the colour order listed above, mixing one colour at a time: pink for the roses and buds, violet, red, etc **(b)**. For help with painting sprays, see page 21. As an extra touch, add a rose and bud to the inside of the box .

b

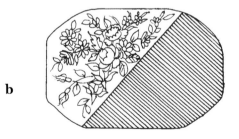

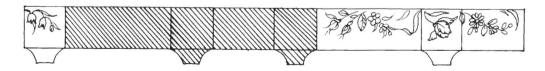

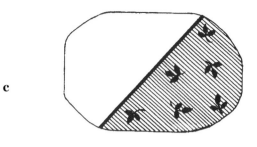

c

Mix black with icing sugar and water (1 part sugar, 2 parts black) and pen tiny dots in the yellow centre of the flowers. Sign your work under the base and fire at 800°C/1470°F.

Shake the matt gold thoroughly before painting the gold leaf design over the groundlay with your gold brush, adding a line around the base and to separate the groundlay and flowers **(c)**. Fire at 700°C/1290°F.

Burnish the gold.

Hexagonal box

This design also involves etching and lustre, but is easier to execute than you might expect.

'I relief' is normally used for modern raised work. Unlike normal relief it is matt and rough to the touch, so it will take bright gold but not matt gold. Here we are using it thinly, so it is not in fact in relief.

Materials needed
turpentine, fat oil, full cream milk
green (acetone based) resist, resist brush
acetone (nail varnish remover) to rinse brush
I relief, red lustre, brush kept for lustre
bright gold, gold brush
rose brush No. 3, long pointer No. 2,
small long square floppy brush
tracing paper, graphite paper (optional)
graphite pencil, marking pen,
sponge, tooth picks, cotton balls
colours in order of use: black, yellow, pink,
violet, red, light blue, light golden brown, dark
brown, light green, dark green, blue green

Cut a circle of tracing paper, 3.5 cm in diameter, centre it on the lid and draw round it with the pencil.

Apply green resist around the circle **(a)** and on the three alternate panels **(b)** around the base which will be painted with lustre, making sure that the centre front panel contains the I relief design.

Mix I relief with a tiny amount of light brown so that it is beige (this is so that you can see where it has been applied in due course). Add milk until it is a very thin cream consistency. Apply quickly with the floppy brush inside the circle and the three non-lustre panels and immediately smooth it over with the sponge. You must work very quickly as the mixture dries extremely fast. I suggest you try first on a tile until you feel confident with the procedure. Repeat on the panels on the base.

When dry, remove the resist and scratch off any excess relief with a tooth pick or dry cotton bud.

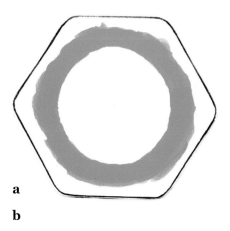

a

b

After the first firing

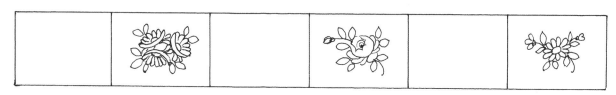

c

Trace or draw freehand the flowers on the base panels and the bird on the lid **(c and d)**.

With a tooth pick, now completely scratch out the designs **(see above)**, pushing away the powder created with a cotton ball so as not to breathe it in.

Fire at 780°C/1435°F.

Mix black with icing sugar and water and pen the bird's beak, eye and legs.

Mix all the other colours with turpentine and fat oil and paint the bird with a light wash, starting at the tail and working up the body, followed by the wing, from the tip to the shoulder.

Paint the flowers and leaves on the base.

With the long pointer add the details to the feathers, leaf veins, shading for flowers, tree and leaves.

Fire at 780°C/1435°F.

d

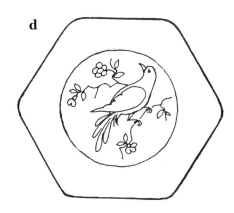

42

After the second firing

With the gold brush carefully paint bright gold over the relief around the designs.

Paint the lustre carefully around the circle on the lid and on the white panels on the base, and sponge it smooth and even.

Fire at 720°C/1328°F.

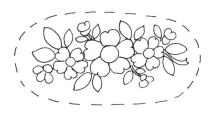

a

b

c

Gold lace box

This is a very simple idea, for any box, and it also requires only one firing. Any piece of lace can be interpreted in this way, the heavier threads being done with a brush, and the background net with a pen.

Materials needed
graphite pencil, marker pen
burnishing gold
pointer brush for gold, pen for gold

Trace or sketch with a pencil the main design on the lid of the box **(a)**, and draw fine parallel pencil lines around it.

With the brush outline the design with gold and draw with the pen the fine grid inside the petals **(b and c)**.

Draw six fine parallel pencil lines around the side of the box base **(d)**, and divide the full length of the side into eight equal sections, so that you can paint with the brush eight circles, equal distances apart.

To make the honeycomb pattern on the lid and sides of the base, make short vertical strokes of gold with the pen between one pair of parallel lines, as indicated in diagram **(d)**. Then add oblique strokes - like pointed roofs - between these vertical strokes and the next parallel line. The point will give you the position for the next set of vertical strokes, and thus the honeycomb pattern will be formed. Continue until the background is complete **(e)**.

Draw a gold diamond with a pen inside each of the double circles **(e)**.

Fire at 780°C/1435°F.

Burnish with sand, fibreglass burnisher or pad.

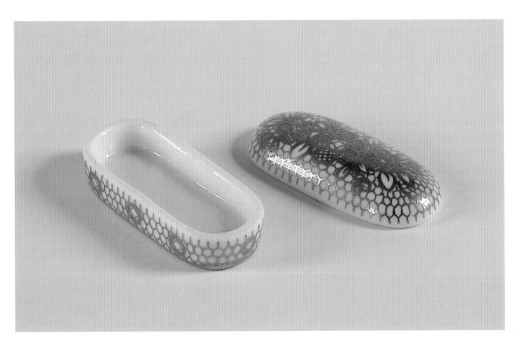

After the firing

d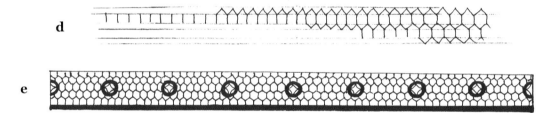

e

45

b

Malachite box

This oblong box was designed to hold two small perfume bottles (see page 19).

Materials needed
open (non drying) medium, fat oil, turpentine peelable resist, icing sugar
square shader brush No. 8, small pointer or tiny square shader, rose brush, long pointer brush, pen
colours in order of use: chrome green, black, emerald green, rose pink, violet, red, light blue, yellow, light golden brown, dark green, light green, blue green

After the first firing

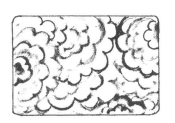

a

Draw a pencil line around the edge of the lid.

Apply resist on the sides of the box lid, where it is to remain white.

Mix chrome green and black separately, both with icing sugar and water.

With the pen, make rosettes, overlapping each other at random, in different shades of green and black by mixing the two colours **(a)**.

Using the small pointer or square shader, apply a wash (thin paint) of different greens and in varying widths between the pen lines.

Mix emerald green with the open medium and with the larger square shader cover the whole of the dried design with a feathery stroke.

Fire at 800°C/1470°F.

46

Draw freehand or trace the flowers, following the sample design **(b)**.

Mix pink with turpentine and fat oil, and paint the roses and buds around the box base. Continue with the other flowers using the colours in the order above. With black mixed with icing sugar and water pen tiny dots in the centres of the flowers, and sign your work. Fire at 800°C/1470°F.

Paint a gold line around the malachite of the lid and at the base of the box.

Fire at 730°C/1346°F if over the malachite, or 780°C/1435°F if on white. Burnish the gold.

Left: after the second firing

Pillar box with cartouches

If you feel that having four bouquets makes the flowers very small, it would be equally nice with three or even two oval cartouches. Alternatively adapt the design for a larger box.

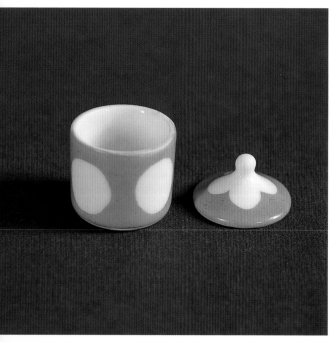

After the first firing

Materials needed
turpentine, fat oil, clove oil, icing sugar
rose brush No. 3, long pointer brush No. 2
gold brush, resist brush, flat brush
graphite paper, graphite pencil, marker pen
peelable resist, sponge
colours in order of use: rose pink, violet, red, light blue, yellow, light golden brown, light green, dark green, blue green, black

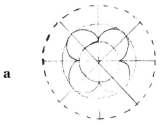

a

Cut a small circle of tracing paper 17.5 mm in diameter.

Using a paper divider, divide the lid vertically into 8 sections and horizontally into 3 rings. Draw the curves between the vertical and horizontal lines **(a)**.

Using a graphite pencil and paper divider again, divide the lower part of the box vertically into 8. Place the paper stencil under the clasp position, and 4 mm from the base, and draw a line around it with the pencil. Repeat 3 times, at equal intervals, using alternate verticals to position the circle. Paint resist in the circles on the base and within the curved area on the lid **(b)**.

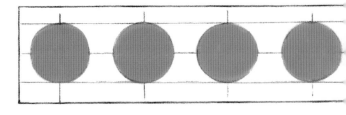

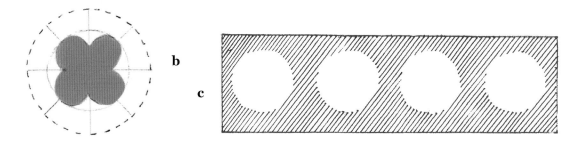

b

c

Mix the chosen groundlay colour with fat oil and turpentine and a few drops of clove oil to slow drying, and paint it on with long strokes of the flat brush in the reserved area. Smooth it over with a sponge.

When it is dry, peel off the resist and clean off any marks on the white area **(c)**. Fire at 825°C/1515°F.

Mix pink with turpentine and fat oil and paint rose buds on the lid and roses on the base **(d and e)**. Follow with the other colours in order, to build up the sprays in the 4 circular areas **(right)**, ending with black. For help with flowers, see page 21. Sign your work.

Fire at 800°C/1470°F.

After the seond firing

d

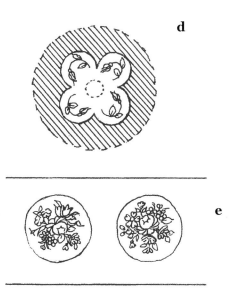

e

 **f**

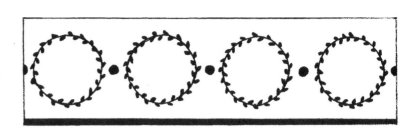 **g**

Paint a thin line of gold on the edge of the curves on the lid, and a swagged garland of tiny leaves **(f)** in the groundlay area. Paint a garland around each cartouche on the base, large gold dots between the cartouches **(g)** and the knob on the lid. Paint a gold line round the base. Fire at 700°C/1290°F.

Burnish gold with sand, burnisher or pad.

Sea shell purse

Shells are a welcome change from flowers, and fit happily on this unusual box design.

Materials needed
turpentine, fat oil, clove oil, resist, matt gold rose brush No. 3, long pointer brush No. 2, gold brush, resist brush, small flat synthetic brush tracing paper, graphite paper, graphite pencil, marker pen, sponge
colours: turquoise (or any ground colour of your choice), pink, yellow, red, light golden brown, dark brown, blue, violet, light green, dark green

Cut an oval from tracing paper, centre it on each side of the box and draw round it.

Apply resist on the inside of the oval, where it is to remain white **(a)**.

Mix your groundlay colour with turpentine, fat oil and a few drops of clove oil to slow drying, and paint both sides of the box with long strokes of the synthetic brush. Smooth the paint over with the sponge.

When dry, lift off the resist and fire at 825°C/1515°F.

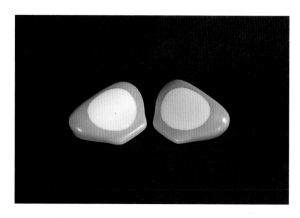

After the first firing

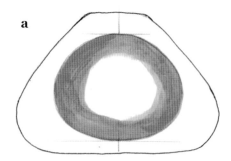

a

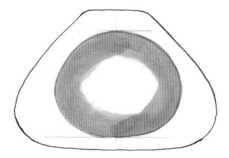

Draw or trace and transfer the shell designs on to the box sides **(b)**.

Mix the colours with turpentine and fat oil and, starting with the main shells, paint the whole design lightly.

Fire at 800°C/1470°F.

With the same colours, freshly mixed or resurrected with the addition of turpentine, add details. Because the box is decorated on both sides, I have not signed it, but if you wish to do so you could sign beneath the design, near the base, or inside, at this stage.

Fire at 780°C/1435°F.

b

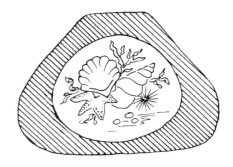

After the second firing

With matt gold and the long pointer gold brush paint a line around each oval, add the marine creatures and seaweed over the colour ground **(c)**, and a surprise one inside the purse if you wish. Fire at 700°C/1290°F.

c

Fruit basket

After the first firing

A charming basket with a surprise inside - tiny bunches of cherries.

Materials needed
turpentine, fat oil, icing sugar
long pointer brush, pen and nib
tracing paper, graphite paper (optional),
graphite pencil, marker pen
reusable putty-like adhesive
colours in order of use: yellow light golden brown, red, violet, light green, dark green, medium brown, dark brown, black

Trace or draw the fruit in an oval in the centre of the lid **(a)**.

Mix all the colours with turpentine and fat oil, except for the last three.

Using the long pointer, paint the fruit lightly: a yellow lemon, light green and pink pear, apples in green with a touch of red and yellow, violet grapes and light brown nuts. Add the leaves in light and dark green.

a

Paint tiny cherries and their leaves at random inside the box **(b and top)**.

Fire at 800°C/1470°F.

b

54

Strengthen the colours of the fruit if necessary, using fresh or resurrected paint - add a little turpentine.

With the graphite pencil draw about four circular lines around the lid and about seven around the base **(c)**, representing the rings of basketweave.

I suggest you now use an adhesive putty to stick the lid and the base on to a tile, as they are very difficult to hold while painting.

Mix medium and dark brown paint separately with turpentine and fat oil and paint firstly the medium brown in circles round the lid and base, leaving a slight gap between the rings. When dry, scratch out regular vertical lines and paint these dark brown **(d)**. Add shading in dark brown to one side of each rectangular section of the basketweave, and on the curves on the edges of the lid and top and bottom of the base.

Mix black with icing sugar and water and sign your work.

Fire at 800°C/1470°F.

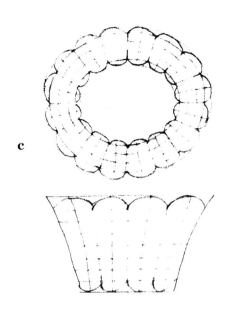

c

d

Dragon box

A touch of the orient, and a rich, royal red.

Materials needed
turpentine, fat oil, clove oil, icing sugar
flat synthetic brush, sponge
long pointer, gold brush
tracing paper, graphite paper, marker pen
matt gold, gold brush, burnisher
reusable adhesive putty, spare tile
colour: red

Mix some of the red powder with icing sugar and water and sign under the base.

Stick the lid by its rim to the tile with the adhesive putty, as you will not be able to hold it while completing the painting.

Mix red with turpentine and fat oil, and a few drops of clove oil to delay drying, and cover the whole of the lid with long strokes of the flat brush.

Smooth it over with the sponge, avoiding any thickness. Repeat on the base, which is easier to hold.

Clean off any smudges of paint and fire at 780°C/1435°F.

If the colour is not deep enough, give the box another coat and fire again at 780°C/1435°F.

Above: after the first firing

Trace the dragon **(a)** and the small designs for the base **(b)** and transfer to the box lid and sides with graphite paper.

b

a

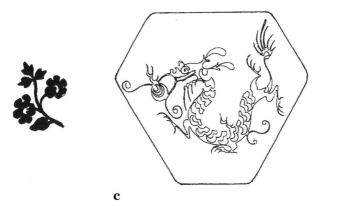

c

Paint the designs with gold, and add bamboo and leaves **(c)** inside if you wish **(left).**

Finish with a gold line round the base. Fire at 700°C/1290°F.

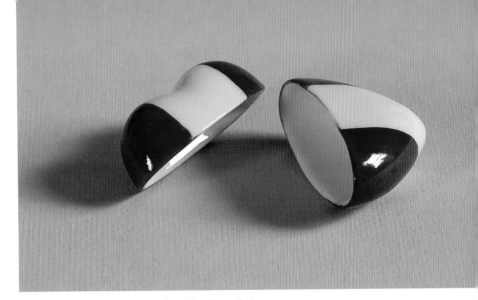

Heart box

The perfect love token

After the first firing

a

b

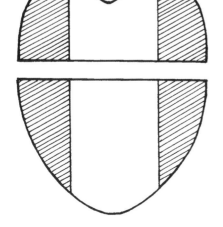

Materials needed
turpentine, fat oil, clove oil
matt gold, icing sugar, resist
rose brush No. 3, long pointer No. 2, gold brush
resist brush, flat synthetic brush
graphite pencil, pen, permanent marker pen
cosmetic sponge, burnisher
colours in order of use: groundlay colour, rose
pink, violet, red, light blue, yellow, light golden
brown, dark green, light green, blue green,
black.

Draw the vertical parallel lines separating the groundlay from the white area.

Apply resist on the inside of these lines **(a)**.

Mix your chosen colour (this is elderberry) with turpentine and fat oil and a few drops of clove oil and apply rapidly to the reserved area with long strokes of the flat brush.

Smooth it over with quick little pats of the sponge. For help with groundlay, see p. 17.

When dry, peel off the resist and clean up any smudges **(b)**.

Fire at 825°C/1515°F.

c

Trace the flower panel design **(c)** and transfer to the box.

Paint the flowers, mixing one colour at a time, starting with the roses, then the vioet tulip and daisies, and so on. For help with flower sprays, see p. 21.

Mix black with icing sugar and water and pen tiny dots around the centres of the daisies, and sign your work inside the lid.

Fire at 800°C/1470°F.

Shake the matt gold thoroughly and, using the long pointer brush, paint the lines along the edge of the panel and the dots on the groundlay **(d)**.

Fire at 700°C/1290°F.

d

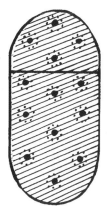

After the second firing

61

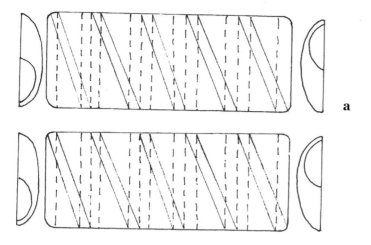

a

Razor shell box

This box shape reminds me of the razor shells we sometimes find on the beach. Its charm lies in the fresh blue ribbon wrapped round it.

Materials needed
turpentine, fat oil, icing sugar, re-usable putty adhesive, spare tile
rose brush No. 3, long pointer No. 2
pen, graphite pencil, marker pen
colours in order of use: light blue, rose pink, violet, dark green, light green, blue green, black

Measure and divide both parts of the box as shown in **(a)**, and draw the diagonal ribbon with the pencil, not forgetting the curved ends.

Stick the two parts on a tile with adhesive putty, as you will find them very difficult to hold while painting. (You can leave them stuck to the tile as the adhesive will turn to powder in the kiln, or lift them off with a palette knife.)

Mix light blue with sugar and water and pen tiny blue dots along both edges of the ribbon.

Mix the same blue powder with turpentine and fat oil and fill in the ribbon with a very light wash, using the long pointer.

Fire at 800°C/1470°F.

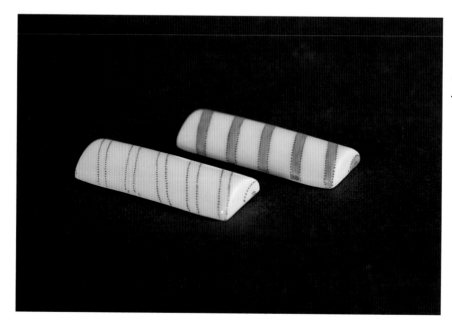

After the first firing

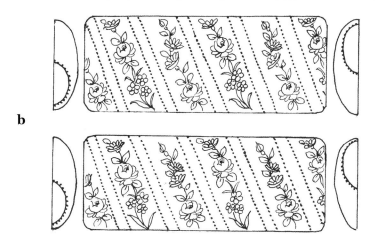

b

Draw the design freehand on the lid and base **(b)**.

Mix rose pink with turpentine and fat oil and paint the roses and buds with the rose brush.

Mix the other colours in turn and paint the daisies and forget-me-nots, adding one or two inside if you wish, and the rest of the flowers. For help with flowers see p. 15.

Fire at 780°C/1435°F.

Golden egg

I like the simplicity of this piece: gold on white is very elegant.

Materials needed
turpentine, fat oil, icing sugar, matt gold
gold brush, long pointer brush, marker pen,
pen and nib
tracing paper, graphite paper, graphite pencil,
reddish brown colour

Trace the design and transfer to the box using the graphite paper, or draw freehand **(a)**.
  Fill in the outlines with a flat coat of matt gold.
  Paint a bird or flower inside the box if you wish.
  Fire at 780°C/1435°F.

If the gold looks even, proceed to the next stage, but if not, paint on another coat of gold and fire again at 780°C/1435°F.
  Do not burnish; it will give a better grip for the next layer of colour.
  Mix the brown with turpentine and fat oil and paint the details of feathers, leaves, etc. with the long pointer **(b and right)**. If you have difficulty making fine lines with the brush, use a pen instead and the icing sugar and water mix (2 parts colour, 1 part sugar)
  Mix the same reddish brown with icing sugar and water and sign your work under the base.
  Fire at 780°C/1435°F.

Burnish with sand, fibreglass burnisher or pad.

After the first firing

64

a

b

Violin case and violin

Everyone will fall in love with this box - wait for the 'Ah!' of surprise when you open the box to reveal the violin.

Materials needed
turpentine, fat oil, icing sugar
long pointer brush, rose brush No. 3
tracing paper, graphite paper, graphite pencil, pen and nib
matt gold, gold brush
colours in order of use: light blue, rose pink, violet, yellow, light golden brown, medium brown, dark brown, light green, dark green, black

Trace or draw the design on the lid **(a)**, base **(b)** and violin **(c)**.

Mix light blue with icing sugar and water and pen tiny dots along each side of the ribbon on the lid and the base.

Mix with turpentine and fat oil, and paint lightly in the following order, without details: violet for the tambourine; light brown for the bassoon; yellow for the rings around the bassoon and the discs around the tambourine; medium brown for the recorder, and a very light shading on the top of the mandolin; dark brown for the mandolin (no strings); grey outline and shading of manuscript on the lid and base; light blue for the forget-me-not on the violin, and you can add one or two inside the case if you wish; light blue wash for the ribbon on the box, pink for all the roses and buds, not forgetting one on the violin; dark green for the rose leaves and buds, and all the stems; light green for the forget-me-not leaves; yellow centres for the forget-me-nots, underlined with light brown.
Fire at 800°C/1470°F.

With the same colours again, add shading where required, paint the strings on the mandolin with dark brown, and paint (or pen with the water mixture) grey musical notes on the manuscripts.

Mix black with icing sugar and water and add one dot inside each forget-me-not. Sign your work on the base.
Fire at 780°C/1435°F.

With gold, paint the strings, the sides and the 'S' shaped frets on face of the violin, and a gold line at the base of the violin case.
Fire at 780°C/1435°F.

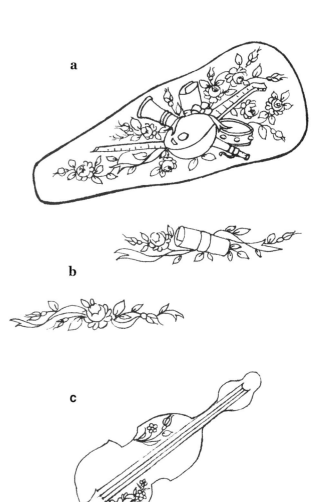

a

b

c

Left: after the first firing

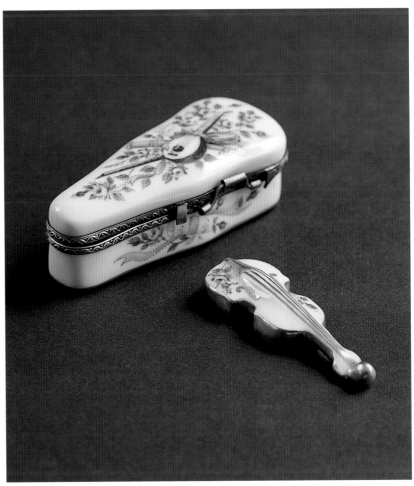

*The violin is complete
with golden strings.*

Stamp box

This box was designed for practical use - the sloping compartments hold postage stamps, and with its design of flowers and an exotic bird it would grace any desk!

Materials needed
turpentine, fat oil, icing sugar, matt gold
rose brush No. 3, gold brush, long pointer brush
pen, marker pen
tracing paper, graphite paper and pencil
colours: pink, violet, yellow, red, light blue, light golden brown, dark brown, light green, dark green, blue green, black

a

After the first firing

68

b

Draw a circle on the lid for the central design. Now draw freehand or trace and transfer to the lid and sides the whole design **(a and b)**, except for the central wreath.

Start with the birds. Mix black with icing sugar and water and pen in the eyes, beak and legs.

Mix yellow, light brown, pink, red, light blue, violet, dark brown and blue green, all at the same time, with turpentine and fat oil.

Starting at the tail, paint with the long pointer in a light wash the various colours on the body, then the wings, starting at the tip, following the colour photograph.

Next paint the branches with dark brown.

Now, remix the colours with a drop of turpentine if they have dried and paint the roses and buds with the rose brush, and the other flowers. See p. 21 for help with painting flowers. Mix light green and dark green and paint the leaves around the birds.

Finish with the black dots on the yellow centres and sign your work under the base.

Using the gold brush, put a series of small gold dots to mark the circle around the bird **(left)**. Fire at 800°C/1470°F.

With the same colours used on the first coat, paint the details on the birds.

With matt gold and the gold brush paint the wreath of small leaves around the circle and a gold line around the base of the box.

Fire at 780°C/1435°F.

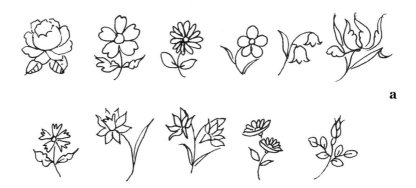

a

Egg pendant

This all-over pattern is reminiscent of the chintz designs on decorated china popular in Victorian tea rooms.

Materials needed
turpentine, fat oil, icing sugar
rose brush No. 3, long pointer No. 2, gold brush
pen, matt gold
colours in order of use: pink, violet, red, light blue, yellow, light golden brown, light green, dark green, black

Stick the two parts of the box on a tile with re-usable adhesive putty.

Mix dark green with icing sugar and water and, using the drawings **(a)** pen lots of flowers at random to fill both halves of the egg **(b and below left)**.

Fire at 800°C/1470°F.

Now mix each colour in turn with turpentine and fat oil and fill your penned outlines, making sure that the colours are evenly balanced over the egg.

Fire at 800°C/1470°F.

After the first firing

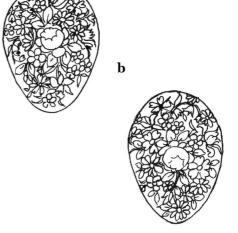

b

After the second firing

Paint gold inside both halves with the gold brush, totally covering the white surface of the egg.

Turn the halves over and carefully stick the rims to the tile with adhesive putty.

Now very steadily fill the background spaces around your flowers with gold, using the gold brush. (You can paint the background with another colour instead of gold, if you wish.)

Fire at 780°C/1435°F.

Etui

Etui is the French word for needle case, which is what immediately came to my mind when I first saw this box. The cornflower design is a traditional Nyon (Swiss) porcelain decoration.

Materials needed
turpentine, fat oil, clove oil, resist, icing sugar
flat synthetic brush, long pointer brush No. 2
graphite pencil, marker pen
paper divider, sponge, matt gold, gold brush,
burnishing sand or pad
colours in order of use: royal blue, dark pink
(American beauty), light green, dark green

After the first firing

Using a paper divider, mark eight divisions with the marker pen on the top and bottom of the box. With the pencil draw the vertical lines separating the panels on lid and base and continue them to meet at the centre of the lid.

Paint masking fluid on 4 matching panels on lid and base, starting at the front **(a and b)**.

Mix the royal blue with turpentine and fat oil, plus a few drops of clove oil to slow drying, and using the flat brush paint the reserved panels. Smooth it over with the sponge.

When dry, peel off the resist, clean off any smudges and fire at 825°C/1515°F.

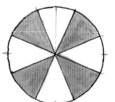

a

b

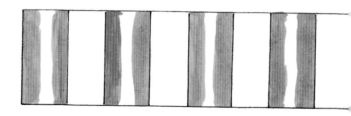

c

d

After the second firing

Mix royal blue with turpentine and fat oil and, using the long pointer, paint 3 cornflowers **(c)** on each panel, top and bottom, followed by smaller ones with two and one petal flowers on the lid **(d)**.

Use light green to paint the leaves and then dark green for stem and veins.

Mix royal blue and dark green with sugar and water and sign your work.

Fire at 800°C/1470°F.

Paint or pen gold dots over the blue ground.

Frame the blue panels with a gold line.

Fire at 700°C/1290°F.

Octagonal box

Why not use a landscape that means a lot to the person you are painting a box for, treated in grey, sepia or their favourite colour? It makes a very special present.

Materials needed
turpentine, fat oil, clove oil
resist, resist brush, flat synthetic brush, sponge
long pointer brush No. 2, rose brush No. 3
tracing paper, graphite paper (optional)
graphite pencil
colours: yellow (or your choice), grey or sepia
matt gold and brush, burnisher

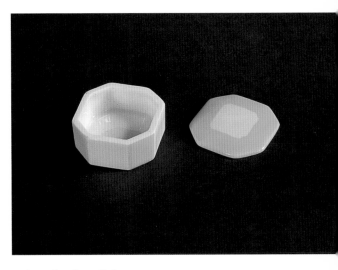

After the first firing

a

Draw vertical lines to mark the divisions on the side and the square panel on the lid.

Paint resist within alternate panels on the sides, starting at the front, and on the lid **(a)**.

Mix yellow or your chosen colour with turpentine and fat oil and a few drops of clove oil, to slow drying, and apply on the reserved areas with the flat brush, not too thickly.

Sponge over quickly, until smooth and even.

When dry, peel off the resist, clean off any smudges and fire at 825°C/1515°F.

After the second firing

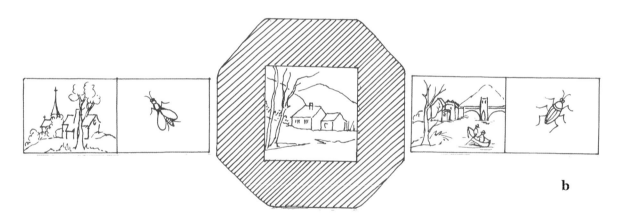

b

Trace or draw in pencil the insects and the scene on the white panels **(b)**.

Mix grey or your preferred colour with turpentine and fat oil and, using the rose brush, start the scene with the sky and background, using very little paint, only a wash, as required.

Work towards the middle ground with a little more colour, and finally to the foreground which should have the strongest value.

For the insects, paint or pen an outline and, with the rose brush, fill this in with a light touch of colour.

Fire at 800°C/1470°F.

Draw the grid with the pencil on the lid, as illustrated, starting with the vertical, then the horizontal, then the diagonal lines **(c)**.

Draw the 4 diamonds on the coloured base panels **(d)**. With the gold brush, paint all the diagonal lines on the lid gold, then add a smaller lozenge within each larger one on the sides. Finally, make a short line inward on each of the inner lozenges to make the star-flower shapes **(d and e)**.

Frame the scene on the lid and the side panels with gold .

Fire at 700°C/1290°F.

76

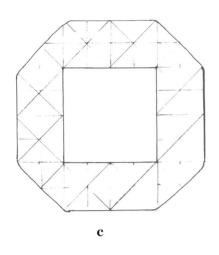

c   d   e

Monochrome oval

It might seem that a monochrome painting is likely to be easier than a polychrome one. It is not so, as particular care must be taken with the contrast between light and dark values, to avoid a flat and lifeless design.

After the first firing

Materials needed
turpentine, fat oil, icing sugar
rose brush No. 3, long pointer brush No. 2
graphite and tracing paper, graphite pencil
pen and nib, marker pen
colours: dark pink (American beauty) or your
own choice

a

Draw or trace and transfer the design on to the lid **(a)** and divide the base in to 10 equal vertical parts **(b)**.

Measure half the height of the base and draw a horizontal line around it, then 2 more, equally spaced 2 mm apart, on either side of this line. Draw the undulating tendril and leaves between the lines **(b)**.

Mix the colour with turpentine and fat oil and, starting with the rose, paint the design lightly. Remember to leave plenty of light - you can always add colour over firings, but once fired you cannot take it away.

Mix some of the same colour with icing sugar and water and pen the tiny dots in the centre of the daisies and on the undulating line on the base. Sign your work beneath the base.

With the original turpentine and fat oil mix, and using the rose brush, add the leaves, omitting the shading.

Fire at 800°C/1470°F.

With the same mix and colour, strengthen the colours where needed, add the shading on the leaves of the base and the dots alternating with these leaves.

Fire at 780°C/1435°F.

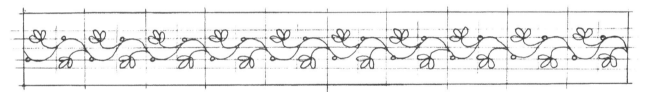

b

b

Butterfly box

A touch of warm summer is suggested by the butterflies and wild flowers.

Materials needed
turpentine, fat oil
rose brush No. 4, long pointer brush No. 2
tracing and graphite paper, graphite pencil, marker pen
colours: black, light blue, yellow, violet, dark brown, grey, pink, light golden brown, light green, dark green, blue green

Trace and transfer using the graphite paper the design to the lid **(a)** and base **(b)**.

Mix the black with turpentine and fat oil and lightly sketch the outline of the butterflies with the long pointer, making the bodies a little darker.

Mix the other colours and with the rose brush paint the light blue wash and a touch of yellow on the wings of the butterfly on the lid. Use dark brown and violet very thinly on the butterflies on the base.

Starting with the large clovers on the lid, paint all the flowers and their leaves and the grasses.

Fire at 800°C/1470°F.

Mix the black as before and paint the fine veins and details on the wings of the butterflies. Sign your work beneath the base.

With pink, add shading to the clover flowers, use dark green for the veins in the leaves, and generally strengthen the painting where you think it is needed.

Fire at 800°C/1470°F.

a

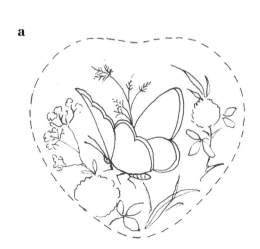

After the first firing

Wooden initial box

You can personalise any box with a decorative initial. There is such a wide selection to choose from - even your computer has a range - but the nicest ones tend to come from old Victorian design pattern books.

Materials needed
marker pen, matt gold, gold brush, burnisher open medium, long square shader
pen, tracing paper, graphite paper and pencil colours in order of use: light golden brown, reddish brown, dark brown, black

Mix separately with the open medium the reddish brown, dark brown and black.

Using the square shader, brush these colours in patches all over the top and base of the box, then blend softly with a feathery stroke.

Use the pen and black to sign your work beneath the base.

Fire at 800°C/1470°F.

Mix the light brown with the open medium and brush smoothly all over the previous coat of colour.

Fire at 800°C/1470°F.

Trace the chosen initial **(a)** and the circle on the lid, with the pencil.

Shake the matt gold thoroughly and paint or pen the initial in gold, and then the evenly spaced dots around the circle **(b)** and the other one on the base **(c)**.

If you are feeling extravagant paint the inside of the box completely with matt gold.

Fire at 700°C/1290°F and burnish the gold.

a

After the first firing

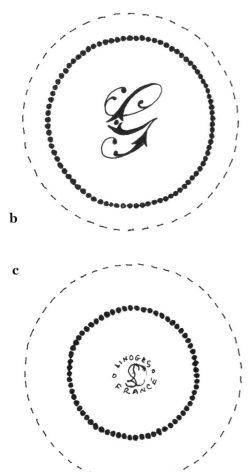

b

c

Glossary

banding wheel (also called a turntable, whirler or lining wheel). A rotating, flat-topped disc on a stand, used to help the application of lines or other decoration on circular pieces.

bone china milk-white glazed porcelain composed of china clay, bone and feldspar.

burnishing rubbing fired matt gold with fine sand or a burnishing pad to make it shine.

burnishing gold *see* gold.

burnishing pad a special, slightly abrasive sponge pad used for burnishing matt gold.

burnishing sand very fine sand, used on a damp cloth to polish matt gold.

cartouche a space reserved in the groundlay for a design. It usually has a decorative border.

closed medium a quick-drying medium.

clove oil a distillation from the clove plant used to delay the drying speed of a painting medium when added to the colour.

dividers circles made of paper or card with divisions into 2, 3, 5, etc, equal parts to help the planning of regular patterns of decoration.

fat oil turpentine which has been thickened by exposure to the air for long periods. It is used as a medium for on-glaze painting.

gold paint bright gold with a pure gold content is used to give the finishing touch to the decorated ware. It has a shiny surface when fired. Matt gold, also known as burnishing gold, is real gold mixed with a medium. The gold content is higher than in bright gold. It has a dull finish and requires polishing after firing.

gold thinners a liquid used to thin down gold when it gets sticky.

groundlay an even application of opaque colour as a background. Also called grounding.

groundlay oil thick fat oil.

marbling veining or painting in imitation of marble .

masking fluid also called resist or peel resist. A latex fluid which is painted on those parts to be reserved in white in a coloured background. It dries to a flexible skin which is peeled off before firing.

matt gold *see* gold.

medium a liquid with which dry colour is mixed before use.

monochrome design one painted in shades of a single colour.

open medium a medium that does not dry.

painting pigments (more properly called on-glaze enamel) colour for application, in a suitable medium, to the glazed surface of ware.

palette a tile or piece of thick glass, suitable for mixing the china-painting colours.

palette knife spatula for grinding and mixing paint on the palette.

peel resist *see* masking fluid.

pipette a dropper, enabling the medium to be added to the paint in controlled quantities. (Some medicine bottles come equipped with droppers.)

polychrome design one painted in many colours.

porcelain fine vitreous ceramic ware made with kaolin, quartz and feldspar, with a slightly grey-tinged glaze.

pouncer a pad made with two layers of silk

over a ball of cotton wool. Used to smooth groundlay oil.

quick-drying medium (also called closed medium) when added to enamel gives a very short painting time before drying. Essential for the one-firing decoration technique.

relief enamel, also called a raised enamel. A white enamel containing clay, used to produce raised designs.

resist *see* masking fluid.

rose brush short pointer brush shaped like a grain of wheat, made of red squirrel hair set in a quill. Used to paint stylized roses and other flowers with broad petals.

methylated spirit, or alcohol. A fluid for cleaning away grease before painting.

stabilo pencil soft graphite pencil used to trace designs on to ware.

stencil shape or design made on tracing paper to be transferred on to the ware.

sugar icing (or powdered) sugar, mixed with enamel (in ratio 1:2) and water, makes a good quick-drying paint for use with a pen.

turpentine genuine turpentine is oil extracted from the pine tree, and used when grinding on-glaze paint colours. It is quick drying.

Suppliers, Associations and Journals

All organisations tend to change with time, but I have listed here tried and tested addresses for suppliers. I suggest that you ask your supplier about magazines and associations which are current in your area.

Britain

Held Products Ltd
Schura School House, Burnt Yates, Ripley, Harrogate, HG3 3EF
tel: 01423.770183
e-mail: sales@held.co.uk
web: www.held.co.uk

Westfield House
North Avenue, Wakefield, WF1 3RX
tel: 01924.360625
e-mail: supplies @ westfieldhouse. co.uk
web: www.westfieldhouse.co.uk
Also publishes *The British Porcelain Painter*

France

Ceradel
Z.I.N, 17-23 Frederic Bastiat, B.P. 1598, 87022 Limoges, Cedex 9
tel: 05 55 35 02 35
e-mail: ceradel-socor@wanadoo.fr
web: www.ceradel.fr/com

Italy

Hobbyceram
Via P. L. Palestrina 13, 20124 Milano
tel: (02) 66981271
e-mail: info@hobbyceram.com
web: www.hobbyceram.com/4k

Switzerland

Cercle Artistique des peintres sur Porcelaine
Rue de l'evolve 50, CH-2000 Neuchatel
tel: 41(0) 32 731 19 86
e-mail: info@capp-porcelaine.ch
web: www.capp-porcelaine.ch

Germany

Porzellan Palette
Gertigstrasse 15
D-22303, hamburg
tel: 004940 270 02 33
e-mail: porzellanpalette@aol.com
web: www.porzellanpalette.com

United States

IPAT (International Porcelain Artists and Teachers Inc) is a non-profit educational organisation maintaining an office (and museum) at 204 East Franklin Street, Grapevine, Texas 76051. It has a worldwide membership and publishes *Porcelain Artist*. International conventions and exhibitions are held biennially, as are regional conventions.
web: www.ipat.org

WOCP (The World Organization of China Painters) includes china painters of all abilities, suppliers and collectors. It publishes *The China Painter* and holds national and regional conventions and shows. For more information and details of local groups contact the headquarters
tel: (405) 521.1234, or fax: (405) 521.1265.
e-mail: .wocporg@the shop.net
web: www.theshop.net/wocporg

Maryland China
54 Main Street, Reisterstown, MD 21136
tel: (410) 833 5559, (800) 638 3880
e-mail: info@marylandchina.com
web: www.marylandchina.com

Rynne China Company
222 West Eight Mile Road, Hazel Park, MI 48030
tel: (248) 542 9400, fax: (248) 542 0047
e-mail: info@rynnechina.com
web: www.rynnechina.com

Freddi's China Closet
3573 Hayden Avenue, Culver City, CA 90323- 2412
tel: (310) 836 2660
e-mail: freddischina@earthlink.net

Mr & Mrs of Dallas, inc
8428 Highway 121N, Melissa, TX 75454
tel: (972) 837 2600
e-mail: mrandmrs@texoma.net
web: www.mrandmrsofdallas.com

Australia

Gold Coast China Painting Supplies
PO Box 2839, Nerang, Queensland 4211
tel: (07) 5594 4269
fax: (07) 5579 8269
e-mail: erdunn@bigpond.com

New Zealand

Western Potters Supplies
Unit 4 Linwood Park, 43a Linwood Avenue
Mt Albert, Auckland
tel: 0064 9 815 1513
fax: 0064 9 815 1515
e-mail: quentin.w@hug.co.nz

Index